JavaScript

*What EVERY Beginner Needs
to Know*

Table of Contents

Introduction

I would like to thank you and congratulate you for purchasing the book: *JavaScript*.

This book contains the steps and strategies that you are going to need in order to master JavaScript so that you can make your personal life easier and even earn yourself a better job than you already have.

JavaScript is going to be useful in more than just programming, even though that is what JavaScript is typically used for.

Here is an inescapable fact: JavaScript is used in a lot of what you use every day. Many programs that you may take for granted were created through the use of Java. If not, then they have at least some sort of tie or affiliation to Java.

Additionally, if you want to master Computer Programming, we have guides on **Python and SQL** as well. And for anyone interested in surfing the Internet anonymously, we have books on **TOR and Anonymous Internet Surfing.** And finally, no savvy computer user's arsenal would be complete without a basic understanding of **Hacking** (don't worry it's the good kind); so we have books on that fascinating topic as well!!

Check out our Amazon author page (https://www.amazon.com/author/ma1982) to find resources such as this- AND MORE:

https://www.amazon.com/dp/B01MSLLTYR

https://www.amazon.com/HACKING-Beginner-Penetration-Security-Programming-ebook/dp/B01N8ZF5F4

If you check out our Programming Library, you WILL increase your earning capacity and marketability at any company dramatically. You will confidently walk into any interview knowing that your skill sets **will be valued** and you have something unique to bring to the table. So don't miss out!!

It is now time for you to become an expert on Java and gain an understanding of all that it can do for you! Let's dive in.

Chapter 1:
What is JavaScript?

JavaScript is one of the languages that are used in programming when designing web pages so that they are interactive with their users. JavaScript will run off of the user's computer and not require any download consent. Usually, JavaScript is used for things such as the creation of polls and quizzes.

JavaScript is known as a high level program that is going to be dynamic, interpreted, and untyped. It is actually one of the three technologies that helps to make up the content that you see on the Internet. Many of the major websites, emails, and web browsers that do not have plug-ins are going to run off of JavaScript.

JavaScript has first class functions that are prototype based thus making it a multi-paradigm language that is going to support object-oriented programming styles. The program has API for when you working with texts, dates, and regular expressions that are not going to include input and output like networking or storage.

There are some strong outward similarities of Java and JavaScript, but they are two different languages that are going to influence the programming in different ways.

JavaScript is not only web-based, but it can be used for creating PDF files, desktop widgets, and site-specific browsers. The new virtual machines are faster thanks to the JavaScript platforms that are built on them. This has increased the popularity of JavaScript for the web applications on the server side.

With the client side, JavaScript has always been known as an interpreted language. However, the more recent browsers it performs a just in time compilation of the browser.

JavaScript can also be used for creating games, desktops, and even mobile applications. Along with that, you can create a server side network that is going to use run-time environments.

JavaScript and jobs

As mentioned above, JavaScript is used for many things. If you have the time and patience to master JavaScript, then you are going to be making yourself a valuable asset to your business.

JavaScript is going to help when you are creating PDF files that have to be sent around the office, or when you have to redesign the company website. If your company is trying to get more of an outreach to the younger generation, then you can use JavaScript in order to create a mobile app that is going to go straight to a Smartphone.

Chapter 2:
The Basics of JavaScript

Where to place it

- JavaScript is not HTML, so when creating JavaScript code, you will need to allow the browser to know that you are entering JavaScript into an HTML page.

- Your function for this will be <script>

- When using <script> type = "text/javascript"> <script> the page is going to know where the JavaScript code starts and ends.

Example:

<html>

<head>

<title> My JavaScript Page </title>

</head>

<body>

<script type = "text/javascript">

Alert ("Welcome to my world!!!");

</script>

</body>

</html>

- Whenever you see the word alert, you are going see an alert box appear on your screen. To proceed, you are going to want to select "Ok" on this box.

- To enter in the alert command, you want the browser to recognize the command as JavaScript.

- If the <script> is not entered, then the browser is going to assume that what you have entered is nothing more than regular text and proceed to write it out on your screen.

- JavaScript can be entered in both <head> and<body> of the HTML document.

- It is recommended to keep as much of your code in the <head> section.

The First Script

- Before you can make your first program, you should know a few more things besides placing your codes between <script>.

- First, JavaScript lines are going to end with semicolons

  - All your JavaScript can be placed in one line without destroying how it performs

  - But, this will destroy how your script looks.

- Place you text inside of quotations.

  - If you forget to place your text inside of quotes, then your script will be read as variables.

- Capitals are different from lowercase

  - When writing script, the capitals should only be placed in their correct places and nowhere else or your script will be messed up.

Example:

```
<html>

<head>

<title> My JavaScript Page </title>

</head>

<body>

<script type = "text/javascript">

</script>

Document.write ("Welcome to my world!!!");

</script>

</body>

</html>
```

- The document..write is going to communicate with the browser that is inside the parentheses should be placed into the document.

- Your output will be similar to what you will get in Python. Welcome to my world!!!

Example:

```
<html>

<head>

<title> My JavaScript Page </title>

</head>

<body>

Hello!!! <br>

<script>

Document.write ("Welcome to my world!!!");

</script>

Enjoy your stay...<br>

</body>

</html>
```

Output:

Hello!!!

Welcome to my world!!!

Enjoy your stay...

- JavaScript will write text where script has been placed in the HTML code

- A wide variety of HTML tags can be written with document.write

Capital Letters

- Java does not see the variable myname the same was that it will see MYNAME

Example one:

<html>

<head>

<title> My Page </title>

</head>

<body>

<script>

myvalue =2;

 myvalue =5;

result = myvalue + myvalue;

document.write(result) ;

```
</script>

</body>

</html>
```

Example two:

```
<html>

<head>

<title> My Page </title>

</head>

<body>

<script>

myvalue =2;

 MyValue =5;

result = myvalue + MyValue;

document.write(result) ;

</script>

</body>

</html>
```

- Because both have different variables, they are going to have different outputs.

- Use the same syntax for all of your variables. Do not mix and match.

- The syntax that you decide to use is not important. What is important is that you choose one and stick with it.

Pop up Boxes

- There are three different pop up boxes that you are going to receive as you go about using JavaScript. The prompt box, the alert box, and the confirm box.

Alert box

- The alert syntax is alert("yourtext");

- "OK" must be clicked in order to proceed with the box.

- This is mostly used when information needs to come through to the user.

- An example is that you want the user to ensure that they know the site contains adult content.

Confirm box

- The confirm box syntax is confirm("yourtext")'

- The user is going to need to click "Ok" or "Cancel"

- This is going to force the user to accept something

- Examples would be confirming their age before they enter the site.

- When the user clicks "Ok" the value is going to be counted as true.

- If the user clicks "Cancel" that means the value will be returned as false.

Example:

If (confirm("Do you agree")) {alert)"You agree")}

Else(alert ("You do not agree")) ;

Prompt box

- The syntax for a prompt box is prompt("yourtext", "defaultvalue");

- Your user is going to be required to click "Ok" or "Cancel" in order to proceed.

- The user is going to have to input a value before they can enter the page.

- Examples would be your name or a password.

- If the "Ok" button is clicked, then the prompt will return to the entry.

- If the "Cancel" box is prompted, then it is going to return as null.

Example:

Username = prompt ("Please enter your name" , "Enter your name here") ;

Chapter 3:
JavaScript's Control Flow Statements

- The narratives that you find in a source file will be executed in the order in which they appear from the top of the page to the bottom.

- But, a control flow statement is going to mess up the flow of operations through decision making, branching, looping, and enabling your program to operate specific chunks of code based on certain conditions.

If-then Statement

- An if than statement is going to be the simplest of any control flow statement.

- The if-then statement will execute the segment of code only in the event that the if is going to be evaluated as true.

Example:

Driver's Ed class will only enable to the breaks to decrease the car's speed only if the car is already in motion.

```
Void applyBrakes() {

// the "if" clause: car must be moving

If (isMoving) {

// the "then" clause: decrease current speed

currentSpeed -- ;

}

}
```

- Should the condition test false, then the control is going to move on to the close of the if-then statement.

- The opening and closing curly brackets are going to be optional, but only if the then clause can be contained inside of a single statement.

```
Void applyBreaks() {

// same as above example, only the curly
brackets are not going to be here.

If (isMoving)

CurrentSpeed -- ;

}
```

- When you make the decision to omit the curly brackets, it is going to be a personal choice. However, if you do omit them, then you are taking the chance of making your code more fragile.

- If your second statement is later, then adding the "then" clause, you can make the mistake of forgetting to add in the curly brackets where they are needed.

- The complier is not going to catch this mistake and thus you will end up with improper results.

If-then-else Statement

- Your if-then-else statement is going to apply a secondary path for the code to be executed in the even that an "if" clause fails.

- Using the earlier example with the car, the if-then-else statement can be applied. So, if the car is not in motion when the breaks are applied then something is going to happen.

- But, you are going to end up getting an error message that will let you know that the car is not moving.

Example

```
Void applyBreakes() {

If (isMoving) {

CurrentSpeed -- ;

} else {

System.err.printin ("The car is not moving!")

}

}
```

Switch Statement

- A switch statement will have a number of execution paths that are going to be possible.

- The switch statement can work with a short, char, byte, and int data type as well as working with enumerated types.

- In this example, an int will be named the month as the value. The code is going to end up displaying the month's name based on which month it is through the use of a switch statement.

Example:

Public class SwitchDemo {

Public static void main (String [] args) {

Int month = 8 ;

String monthString ;

Switch (month) {

Case 1: monthString = "January" ;

Break ;

Case 2: monthString = "February" ;

Break ;

Case 3: monthString = "March" ;

Break ;

Case 4: monthString = "April" ;

Break ;

Case 5: monthString = "May" ;

Break ;

Case 6: monthString = "June" ;

Break ;

Case 7: monthString = "July" ;

Break ;

Case 8: monthString = "August" ;

Break ;

Case 9: monthString = "September" ;

Break ;

Case 10: monthString = "October" ;

```
Break ;

Case 11: monthString = "November" ;

Break ;

Case 12: monthString = "December" ;

Break ;

Default: monthString = "Invalid month" ;

Break ;

}

System.out.println(monthString) ;

}

}
```

- The main part of the switch statement is also known as a switch block

- The comment that is inside of a switch block will be identified with multiple cases or even default labels.

- A switch statement will evaluate the expression before executing all of the statements that succeed the identical label.

- The month's names can also be displayed through the use of an if-then-else statement.

Example:

Int month = 8

If (month == 1) {

System.out.println ("January") ;

} else if (month ==2) {

System.out.println ("February") ;

}

... so on and so forth.

- The if-then-else statement will be used depending on the clarity and the expression that your statement is examining.

- The if-then-else statement is going to test the expressions depending on the conditions and values where a switch statement is only going to test the expression based on single integers, string objects, and enumerated values.

- The break statements are going to terminate the switch statement.

- But, the control flow is going to continue with the first comment that follows a switch block.

- Break statements are vital because if you do not have them, then the switch block is going to end up falling through. So, all statements that are after the identical labels will be executed in the sequence that they fall, despite any of the case labels, up until a break statement is reached.

- The following example is going to show how a statement within a switch block will fall through.

Example

Public class SwitchDemoFallThrough {

Public static void main (String[] args) {

Java.util.ArrayList<String> futureMonths =

```
New java.util.ArrayList<String> () ;

Int month = 8 ;

Switch (month) {

Case 1: futureMonths.add ("January") ;

Case 2: futureMonths.add ("February") ;

Case 3: futureMonth.add ("March") ;

Case 4: futureMonth.add ("April) ;

Case 5: futureMonths.add ("May") ;

Case 6: futureMonths.add ("June") ;

Case 7: futureMonths.add ("July") ;

Case 8: futureMonths.add ("August") ;

Case 9: futureMonths.add ("September") ;

Case 10: futureMonths.add ("October") ;

Case 11: futureMonths.add ("November") ;

Case 12: futureMonths.add ("December") ;

Break ;

Break ;
```

```
Default: break ;

}

 If (futureMonths.isEmpty()) {

System.out.println ("Invalid month number") ;

} else {

For (String monthName : futureMonths) {

System.out.println (monthName) ;

}

}

}

}
```

- Your output is going to be the months August through December

- In the example just shown, the ending break does not have to be placed into the code since the flow is going to vanish from the switch statement.

- A break will be recommended though because it is going to make it simpler for you to modify your code and you will have less of a chance of getting an error message.

- The default section of the code is going to deal with all the values that are not handled by a case section.

- Code can have multiple cases. The following example is going to show that to you.

Example

```
Class SwitchDemo2 {

Public static void main (String[] args) {

Int month = 2;

Int year = 2016;

Int numDays = 0

Switch (month) {

Case 1: case 3: case 5:

Case 7: case 8: case 10:
```

```
Case 12

numDays = 28

break ;

case 4: case 6:

case 9: case 11:

numDays = 31;

break;

case 2:

if ((year % 4 == 0) &&

!(year % 100 == 0))

|| (year % 400 == 0 ))

NumDays = 31;

Else

numDays= 30;

break;

default:

system.out.println ("Invalid month.") ;
```

break ;

}

System.out.println ("Number of Days = " +
numDays) ;

}

}

- Ultimately, your output is going to be 29 because there are 29 days in the second month of the year.

Strings in switch statements

- String objects can be placed into a switch statement.

- When a string is placed in a switch, the expression is going to be compared with another expression that is associated with the case labels.

- For the string to be accepted into the switch, the month case is going to need to be lowercase and anything that is associated with the case labels will need to be lowercase.

Example

Public class StringSwitchDemo {

Public static int getMonthNumber(String month) {

Int monthNumber = 0

If (month == null) {

Return monthNumber ;

}

Switch (month.toLowerCase()) {

Case "January":

monthNumber = 1

break ;

- And you will continue that way until you have written all twelve months out in lower case with the month number that is associated with it.

While and do-while statements

- A while statement will work out the block of statements continually if a particular condition is found to be true.

- The syntax is:

While (expression) {

Statement(s)

}

- A while statement is going to evaluate the expression which will then return a Boolean statement.

- If the expression is evaluated as true, then the while statement will execute the statement or statements that are inside of the while block.

- The while statement is going to continue to test the expression as well as executing the block until the condition is proven false.

Example:

```
Class WhileDemo {

Public static void main(String[] args) {

Int count = 1 ;

While (count < 11) {

System.out.println(" Count is: " + count) ;

Count++;

}

}

}
```

- An infinite loop can be implemented as you use the while statement with the following syntax.

```
While (true){

// your code goes here

}
```

- A do-while statement is also provided by JavaScript.

Do {

Statement(s)

} while (expression) ;

- The main difference that you will notice between a do-while statement and a while statement is that the do-while statement is going to evaluate the expression at the bottom of the loop instead of the one that is at the top.

- Therefore, every statement that is in the do block will be executed at least once.

Example:

Class DoWhileDemo {

Public static void main(String[] args) {

Int count = 1

Do {

System.out.println ("Count is: " + count) ;

Count++;

} while (count < 11) ;

}

}

For Statement

- A for statement is going to provide a compact way to iterate inside of a range of values.

- This is often referred to as "for loop" since it constantly loops until the condition that was set forth has been satisfied.

- The syntax for the for statement is:

For (initialization; termination;

Increment) {

Statement(s)

}

- Before you use a for statement, you should keep in mind:

    o That an increment expression will be invoked after an iteration through the loop. It is acceptable for this to express an increment or decrement of a value.

- o An initialization expression will initialize the loop. It is executed as soon as the loop begins.

- o A termination expression is going to evaluate as false, then the loop is going to be terminated.

Example

```
Class ForDemo {

Public static void main(String[] args) {

For (int i=1 ; i<11; i++){

System.out.println ("Count is: " + i);

}

}

}
```

- Your output is going to be 1 through 10.

- The code will declare that a variable that is within the initialization expression

- The variable scope is going to extend from the declaration to the end of the block as governed by a for statement.

- The for statement is going to be used in the increment and termination expression too.

- Should the variable control a for statement, it will not be needed outside of the loop. It is better to declare the variable in the initialization expression.

- Name i, j, and k will be used for controlling for loops

- When declared in the initialization expression, their life span will be limited and the amount of errors will be reduced.

- There are three expressions that can be used for a "for" loop. But, an infinite loop is going to be created with the following syntax.

// infinite loop

For (; ;) {

// your code goes here

}

- The for statement also has another variation that can be used with iteration. This variation is going to be referred to as enhanced for statements and can be used to make a loop smaller and easier to read.

Example

Int[] numbers = {1, 2, 3, 4, 5, 6, 7, 8, 9, 10};

Class EnhancedForDemo {

Public static void main (String[] args){

Int[] numbers =

{1, 2, 3, 4, 5, 6, 7, 8, 9, 10};

For (int item : numbers) {

System.out.print;n (" Count is : " + item) ;

}

}

}

- The variable item is going to hold the value in the example therefore, your output is going to be 1 through 10 again.

- This variation is recommended when writing out for statements over the general way that a for statement is written out.

Branching statements

Break statements

- A break statement has two different forms, unlabeled and labeled. The unlabeled will be part of the switch statement.

- An unlabeled break will have the ability to terminate a for, while, and do-while loop

Example

Class BreakDemo {

Public static void main(String[] args) {

Int[] arrayofInts =

{ 32, 87, 3, 589,

```
12, 1076, 2000,

8, 622, 127 };

Int searchfor = 12;

Int I;

Boolean fountIt = false;

For (I = 0; I < arrayOfInts . length; i++) {

If (arrayOfInts [i] == searchfor) {

fountIt = true;

break;

}

}

If (foundIt) {

System.out.println("found " + searchfor + " at
index " + i);

} else {

System.out.println (search for + " not in the
array");

}
```

}

}

- The break statement is going to be shown in bold print, termating the loop when it reaches the value that needs to be found.

- Control flow will then transfer to a for loop.

- The output will be found 12 at index 4

- A break that is unlabled is going to terminate the inner parts of a switch, for, while, and do-while statement.

- A labeled break is going to terminate the outside statements.

- The example is going to use nested loops in order to search for values on the two-dimensional array. After the value has been located, the labeled break will terminate the outer "for" loops.

Example

```
Class BreakWithLabelDemo {

Public static void main(String[] args) {

Int[] [] arrayOfInts = {

{ 32, 87, 3, 589 },

{ 12, 1076, 2000, 8 },

{ 622, 127, 77, 955 }

};

Int searchfor = 12

Int I;

Int j = 0

Boolean foundIt = false;

Search:

For (I =0; I < arrayOfInts.length; i++) {

For (j = 0; j < arrayOfInts[i].length;

J++) {

If (arrayOfInts[i][j] == searchfor) {
```

foundIt = true;

break search;

}

}

}

If (foundIt) {

System.out.println("Found " + searchfor + " at " + I + ", " +j);

} else {

System.outprintln(searchfor + " not in the array");

}

}

}

- The output is going to be that 12 was found at 1.

- The labled statement will be terminated by the break statement; it is not going to transfer the flow of control to the label.

- Control flow will be transferred to the statement instantly after the label terminates the statement.

Continue statement

- A continued statement will skip the iteration that is currently in place for the for, while, and do-while loops.

- The form that is unlabeled will skip to the close of parts that are in the inner parts of the loop's body and then evaluate the Boolean expression that is controlling the loop.

- The example that follows is going to show you the directions through a string while counting the number of occurrences for the letter p.

- If the character that is current is not the letter p, then the continue statement will then skip the all of the loop and go to the next letter. Should the letter be p, then the program is going to increment the count.

Example

Class ContinueDemo {

Public static void main(String[] args) {

String searchMe = "Peter Piper picked a " + "peck of pickled peppers";

Int max = searchMe.length();

Int numPs=0;

For (int I = 0; I < max; I++) {

// interested only in p's

If (searchMe.charAt(i) ! = 'p')

Continue;

// process p's

numPs++;

}

System.out.println(found" + numPs + " p's in the string. ");

}

}

- The output is going to be that there are 9 p's inside of the string for this example.

- If you remove the continue statement and run it again there will be 35 p's

- The continue statement that is labeled will skip the current iteration of the outer loop that is marked with a label.

- This next example is going to use two loops that are nested in order to search for a substring inside of a string.

- Two nested loops are going to be required so one has an iterate over the substring and the other over the string that is being searched.

Example

Class ContinueWithLabelDemo {

Public static void main(String[] args) {

String searchMe = "Look for a substring in me" ;

String substring = "sub";

Boolean foundIt = false;

Int max = searchMe.length() –

```
Substring.length();

Test:

For (int I = 0; I <= max; i++) {

Int n = substring.length();

Int j = I;

Int k =0;

While (n -- != 0) {

If (searchMe.charAt(j++) !=
substring.charAt((k++)) {

Continue test;

}

}

foundIt = true;

break test;

}

System.out.println(foundIt ? "Found it" : "Didn't
find it");

}
```

}

Return statement

- A return statement is the ending of the branching statements.

- A return statement is going to exit the method that is most current and then the control flow is going to be returned to the moment the method was first invoked.

- There are two forms for a return statement. The one where the value is going to be returned and the other where the value will not be returned.

- In order to return a value, you are going to put the value after your return keyword.

- The syntax for returning a value is return ++count;

- When a data type returns the value, it has to match the type that the method declared as the return value.

- If a method declares the value bad, use the return form that will not give you a value as a return.

- The syntax for not returning a value is return;

Chapter 4:
Loop Types in Java

- When an operation is repeated, it is considered looping in JavaScript.

- Loops have a series of instructions that will continue the same block of code until a certain condition is returned as true or false depending on what is needed.

- In order to govern the loops, you will need to have a conflicting variable that will increment or decrement every time the loop is repeated.

- JavaScript is going to support two different loop statements, the for loop and the while loop.

- For statements are going to perform the best when they are used in a loop that set number of times.

- Additionally, if you can use a break and a continue statement inside of a loop.

For Loop

- A for loop is going to be executed up until a specific condition is returned as false.

- The syntax is going to be the same as it is in any other languages.

- A for loop is going to have three different arguments.

For (initialization; condition; increment)

{

// statements

}

- A loop statement is going to be executed if:

    o The statement is executed and the control returns to step 2

    o The condition expression has been evaluated and the condition for the value is true. The loop statement will be executed only if the value of the condition is false, then the loop is going to be terminated.

- The beginning expression is executed. This expression is going to initialize one or even several loop go through the syntax which will allow an expression of any degree and complexity.

- A definition for an increment has been updated and executed.

Example

```
<script type = "text/ javascript">

Document.write("<hl>Multiplication table</hl>");

Document.write("table border = 2 width = 50%");

For (var I = 1; I <=9; i++) { //this is the outer loop

Document.write("<tr>");

Document.write("<td>" +I + "</td>");

For (var j = 2; j <= 9; j++) { // inner loop

Document.write ("<td>" +I *j + "</td>";

}
```

Document.write("</tr>");

}

Document.write("</table>");

</script>

- The following example is going to have the for statement that counts the amount of selected options inside of the list

- The for statement is going to declare the variables I and initialize it to zero. I will be checked less than the amount of choices that are selected. If it succeeds, the comment and an increase of I by one after every pass through the loop.

Example

<script type = "text/javascript">

Function howMany (selectItem) {

Var numberSelected = 0

For (var I = 0; I < selectItem.options.length; i++) {

If (slectedItem.options[i] . selected == true)

```
numberSelected++;

}

Return numberSelected

}

</script>

<form name = "selectForm">

<p>Choose some book types, then click the
button below: </p>

<select multiple name = "bookTypes" size = "8">

<option selected> Classic </option>

<option> Information Books </option>

<option> Fantasy </option>

<option> Mystery </option>

<option> Poetry </option>

<option> Humor </option>

<option> Biography </option>

<option> Fiction </option>
```

</select>

<input type – "button" value = "How many are selected?"

Onclick = "alert ('Name of options selected: ' + howMany(document.selectForm.bookTypes)) ">

</form>

- Depending on how many books are selected by the user, the output is going to be different. The output can be anywhere from one to eight with this example.

While Loop

- A while loop is a common loop, but not the most common loop.

- The while statement will repeat the loop as long as the specified condition is evaluated to be true.

- Should the condition be false, then the statement that is inside the loop will stop executing and then the control will pass to the statement that follows the loop.

- The syntax for a while loop is going to be:

While (condition)

{

// statements

}

- This example is going to define a loop that will begin with I = 0 and is going to keep running up until the point in time that I is more than 10. With each statement, I is going to increase by one every time the loop is ran.

Example

```
<script type = "text/javascript">

Var I = 0;

While (i<=10) // output from the value from 0 to 10

{

Document.write(I + "<br>")

I++;
```

}

</script>

- No matter what loop you are writing, you should ensure the conditions of the loop are eventually going to be false. If you do not, then the loop is never going to terminate.

Break and continue statements

- There are times that you may want the loop to start without being constrained by a condition, the statements that are inside the set of brackets will decide when to exit the loop.

- Two statements can be placed inside of a loop. The break statement and the continue statement.

- The break statement is going to terminate the most current while or for loop while continuing to execute the script that is trailing the loop if there is any.

- A continued statement is going to terminate the statement block for a while or for loop and then continue with the loop that has the next starting point.

Example

```
<script type – "text/javascript">

Document.write("<p><b>Example of using the break statement: </b></p>");

Var I = 0;

For (i=0; i<=10; i++) {

If (i==3) {break}

Document.write ("The number is " +i);

Document.write("<br />");

}

Document.write("<p><b> Example of using the continue statement: </b><p>");

Var I = 0

For (I = 0; I <= 10; i++) {

If ( i==3) (continue)
```

```
Document.write("The number is " + i);

Document.write("<br />")

}

</script>
```

Chapter 5:
JavaScript Functions

- A function in JavaScript is going to be a code block that is particularly designed to operate a specific task.

- A function will be executed whenever something calls upon it or otherwise invokes it.

Example

Function myFunction(p1, p2) {

Return p1 * p2;

// you function is going to return the product of p1 and p2

}

JavaScript Function Syntax

- The function is going to be defined by the keyword function.

- The name is going to be followed by a set of parentheses ()

- Function names are gong have digits, dollar signs, underscores, and letters. Essentially they are going to follow the same rules as a variable.

- The set of parentheses are going to include parameter names that will be separated through the use of commas.

- All of the code is going to be performed, but the functions are going to be inside of curly brackets ({})

Example

Function name(parameter1, parameter2, parameter3) {

Code to be executed

}

- The function parameters are going to be the names that are listed inside of the definitions function.

- The arguments for a function are going to be the real values that are accepted by the function whenever it has been invoked.

- The arguments in a function are going to behave as local variables.

Function Invocation

- The code that is located in the function is going to be executed whenever it has been invoked.

- The code can be invoked when:

    o It is automatically invoked or self-invoked.

    o An event occurs such as the user clicking a button.

    o It is invoked from the JavaScript code

Function Return

- As your code comes to a return statement, the function is going to stop functioning.

- When the function is invoked due to a statement, the script is going to "return" to execute any code that appears after the invoking statement.

- A function will often times compute the return value.

- The return value is going to be "returned" back to the original caller.

Example

Var x = myFunction (4, 3); //this function has been called upon and is going to be returned with the value being x.

Function myFunction(a, b) {

Return a * b; // function returns the product of a times be

}

- X is going to be 12 which is going to be your output.

Why functions?

- Functions allow for codes to be reused. The code will be defined once and then it is going to be used many times over.

- The same code is going to be used multiple times with different arguments in order to get different results.

Example

Function toCelsius (Fahrenheit) {

Return (5/9) * (Fahrenheit -32);

}

Document.getElementById("demo").innerHTML = toCelsius(77);

The () Operator used to invoke the function

- When you access the function without the use of parentheses, then your function will return the definition.

Example

Function toCelsius(Fahrenheit) {

Return (5/9) * (Fahrenheit – 32);

}

Document.getElementById("demo"). innerHTML = toCelsius;

Functions used like variable values

- Functions have the ability to be used in the same way that variables are used. They can be used in all types of formulas, calculations, and assignments.

- Instead of using a variable so that you can store the returned value of a function.

Example

Var x = toCelsius(77);

Var text = "The temperature is " + x + " Celsius";

- Functions can be used direction as the variable's value

Example

Var text = "The temperature is " + toCelsius(77) + " Celsius";

Chapter 6:
JavaScript Cookies

What are Cookies?

- Cookies are the data that is going to be stored into small text files onto a computer.

- After a web server sends a web page to a browser, the connection is going to be shut down and the server will forget everything that it knew about the user.

- Cookies were originally invented as a way to solve the problem of "how is information about the user supposed to be remembered?"

  o Whenever the user visits the page, the cookie is going to remember the name of the user.

  o Should the user revisit the site, then the site is going to remember his or her name.

- Cookies are going to be saved in a name value pair.

- A browser is going to request the web page from its server.

- The cookies that belong to the page are going to added into the request when the server is sent to the browser in order for the server to get the proper data to remember various pieces of information about its users.

Creating a cookie with JavaScript

- JavaScript has the ability to create, read, and even delete cookies by using the document.cookie property.

- By using JavaScript, a cookie will be created like this:

Document.cookie = "username = Jon Doe";

- Expiration dates can also be used. However, JavaScript is going to default and the cookie will be deleted as soon as the browser is closed

Document.cookie = "username = Jon Doe; expires = Thu, 18 Jan 2013 12:00:00 UTC";

- with the use of path parameters, the browser will be told exactly which path the cookie will belong to.

- By default, the cookie that was created is going to belong to the page the user is on.

Document,cookie = "username = Jon Doe; expires Thu, 18 Jan 2013 12:00:00 UTC; path =/";

Reading cookies with JavaScript

- JavaScript Cookies are going to be read like this:

Var x = document.cookie;

- The document.cookie is going to end up returning all of the cookies within a single string.

Changing a cookie with JavaScript

- JavaScript allows cookies to be changed in the same fashion that a cookie is created. You are going to use the same syntax.

- The old cookie is going to be overwritten.

Deleting cookies with JavaScript.

- To delete cookies, you have to set the parameter to a date that has already passed so that it expires.

Example

Document.cookie = "username =; expires Fri, 01 Jan 1940 00:00:00 UTC";

- You do not have to choose the particular cookie value whenever deleting cookies

Cookie string

- The document.cookie property is going to look like it is a normal text string, however, it is not.

- If you write out the whole string for this function, you are going to read it out only to see the name value pair.

- When a new cookie is set, then the older cookies will not be overwritten. Instead, the new cookie is going to be added to the document.cookie so that the document.cookie can be read again.

- When you are wanting to find the value of a specific cookie, you are going to need to write a function with JavaScript that will then search for the cookie value instead of the cookie string.

Example of a function set to a cookie

- First the function has to be created so that the name of the user can be stored inside of a cookie

Function setCookie(cname, cvalue, exdays) {

Var d = new Date();

d. setTime(d.getTime() + (exdays * 24 *60 *60 *1000));

var expires = "expires=" + d.toUTCString();

document.cookie = cname + "=" + cvalue + ";" + expires + ";path=/";

- The parameters of the function is going to be the name of the cookie (cname), and the value of that cookie (cvalue), and then the number of days until that cookie will expire (exdays).

- The function is going to set the cookie by adding together the name, value, and expiration inside of the string.

Function to get a cookie

- When a function is created, the return is going to be the value of a particular cookie

Example

Function getCookie(cname) {

Var name = cname +"="

Var ca = document.cookie.split(';');

For (var I = 0; I <ca.length; i++) {

Var c = ca[i];

While (c.charAt(0) == ' ') {

C = c.substring(1);

}

If (c.indexOf(name) == 0 {

Return c.substring(name.length, c.length);

}

}

Return "";

}

- The cookie name is going to be the parameter

- In order to create the variable, you are going to need the name along with the text so that you can search for (cname + "="

- The document.cookie is going to be split on semicolons into what is known as an array and it will be called ca

- The loop through the ca arra will read out every value

- Should the cookie be found, then the return of the value for the cookie will be returned.

- If the cookie is not found, then it will read return "".

Function to check cookies

- If the cookie is set, then a greeting is going to be displayed.

- If the cookie has not been set, then it is not going to display a greeting, instead it will display a prompt box that is going to ask for the name of the user before storing it as the user name cookie for a year through the setCookie function.

Example

Function checkCookie() {

Var username = getCookie ("username");

If (username! = "") {

Alert("Welcome again " + username);

} else {

Username = prompt ("Please enter your name:" , "");

If (username != "" && username != null) {

setCookie ("username", username, 365);

}

}

}

Putting it all together

- This example is going to run the checkCookie() function whenever the page loads.

Example

Function setCookie(cname, cvalue, exdays) {

Var d = new Date();

d.setTime(d.getTime() + (exdays* 24 *60 *60 *1000));

var expires = "expires=" +d.toUTCString();

document.cookie = cname + "=" + cvalue + ";" + expires + ";path=/";

}

Function getCookie(cname) {

Var name = cname + "=";

Var ca = document.cookie.split(';');

```
For( var I = 0; I < ca.length; I++) {

Var c = ca[i];

While (c.charAt(0) == ' ') {

C = c.substring(1);

}

If (c.indexOf(name) == 0) {

Return c.substring(name.length, c.length);

}

}

Return "";

}

Function checkCookie() {

Var user = getCookie("username");

If (user != "") {

Alert ("Welcome again + user);

} else {

User = prompt ("Please enter your name:" , "");
```

```
If (user != "" && user != null) {

setCookie( "username", user, 365);

}

}

}
```

Chapter 7:
Programming Your First
JavaScript Site

In this chapter you are going to learn how to write your own program. It is going to be a simple program that you are going to be able to do over and over again until you get the hang of it. All that is going to matter is that you are getting the hands on experience that you need in order to be able to write your own program.

For this one, you are going to be adding some JavaScript to a web page that already exists. You are going to want to go to www.washington.edu in order to gain some more knowledge on this subject.

By the end of this course, you are going to have the knowledge of:

- How a basic JavaScript syntax will work

- And how a client-side script file will fit into the context of an HTML page.

- First you are going to want to open up a text editor and create a new section. You will create a new section with the subheading of "JavaScript Enhancement." An anchor tag is going to need to be created, you can name it something like "javascript" inside of your subheading.

- At this point in time, you are going to link this to the new section that has come from the relevant item on your home page.

- Add in the code to the heading section, before you end up placing whatever text you are wanting to be placed into the section where your message should go.

```
<script type = "text/javascript">

Function showAlert() {

Var msg = "Your message here";

Alert (msg);

}

</script>
```

- The script mentioned is going to contain a single function, this function is going to be called "showAlert"

- The script is not going to do anything until it has been invoked. When the script is called into response to an even, you are going to need to add in code so that the HTML calls the showAlert script if the user hovers over the link with their mouse.

- To create a new paragraph in the JavaScript Enhancement section, you are going to want to include a link that is going to follow this attribute:

Onmouseover = "showAlert()"

- There are some users that are going to navigate through the links that are located on the page with the use of their keyboard instead of their mouse. A mouse-based event needs to also replicate with the keyboard equivalent.

- A keyboard equivalent of the onmouseover is going to be onfocus.

Onfocus = "showAlert()"

- Make sure that you save all of your work before you load your page into the browser.

- Hover over your link and see what happens.

- Attempt to use the same link through your keyboard keys.

Once you are done, you are going to want to share your page with your friends and family. If you are not to that point yet, then you should keep trying and practicing until you think that you have mastered it.

Chapter 8:
JavaScript Syntax

- The syntax is going to be the set of rules of how JavaScript programs are constructed.

JavaScript Programs

- The computer program is going to have a list of instructions that have to be executed by the computer.

- In a programming language these instructions are going to be called statements.

- JavaScript statements will be separated by using semicolons.

Example

Var x = 5;

Var y = 7;

Var z = x + y;

- In HTML, a JavaScript program is going to be executed by a web browser.

JavaScript Statements

- The JavaScript statement is going to be made up of:

    o Values

    o Comments

    o Expressions

    o Operators

    o And keywords

JavaScript Values

- The syntax in JavaScript is going to be defined by two different value types. The fixed values and the variable values.

- Fixed values are going to be called literals while variable values will be called variables.

JavaScript Literals

- There are some rules for writing fixed variables.

- First, you need to make sure that numbers are written with or without the decimal point.

Example

10.50

1001

- Strings will be text that is written within a set of quotes, whether it be double or single.

Example

"Jane Doe"

'Jane Doe'

JavaScript Variables

- Variables are going to store the data values.

- JavaScript uses var to declare variables

- An equal sign (=) will assign a value to the variable.

Example

Var x;

X = 6;

JavaScript Operators

- JavaScript uses what is known as an assignment operator in order to assign the variables values.

- The assignment operator is the equals sign (=)

Example

Var x = 8

Var y = 9

- The arithmetic operators are going to be used in order to compute values. (+, -. *, /)

JavaScript Expressions

- An expression is going to be a combination of a variety of operators, values, and variables.

- The operators, variables, and values that are found in an expression are going to compute to equal a value.

- The computation process is going to be called an evaluation.

Example

10 * 20

- The evaluation of this example is going to be 200

- An expression also has the ability to contain a variable value.

Example

x * 5

- Values are going to be different data types such as a string or a number.

Example

"Jane" + " " + "Doe"

- The evaluation will be Jane Doe.

JavaScript Keywords

- The keywords are going to be used in order to identify the actions that are needing to be performed.

- The var keyword is going to allow the browser to create a new variable.

Example

Var x = 6 + 8;

Var y = x * 15;

JavaScript Comments

- All the statements that are found in JavaScript are not going to be executed.

- When there are double dashes (//) after a code, or between a /* or even */ it is going to considered a comment.

- The comments are going to be ignored like they are in Python because they are only telling the programmer what is going on with the code. Should a programmer pick up your code again at a later date, they are going to know what you were trying to do with the code and are going to be able to fix what may have gone wrong.

Examples

Var x = 9; //I am going to be executed in order to give you an output.

// var x = 7; //this is not going to be executed because it has a double dash before the code therefore making it to where it is just a comment.

JavaScript Identifiers

- An identifier is going to be a name.

- JavaScript identifiers are used so that variables, keywords, functions, and labels can be named.

- Legal names are going to have the same rules in almost any programming language.

- The first characters are going to have to be a letter, a dollar sign ($) or even an underscore (_)

- Any characters that come after that can be letters, dollar signs, underscores, and digits.

- Numbers are not allowed to be used as the first character. This is so that JavaScript can distinguish an identifier from a number.

Case Sensitive

- The identifiers in JavaScript are going to be case sensitive.

- The variable lastName and lastname are going to be considered two different variables.

Example

lastName = "Mann";

lastname = "Johnson";

- However, VAR and Var are not going to be interpreted as the keyword var.

Camel case

- There are three ways that programmers can join multiple words so that it makes one variable instead of several.

Hyphens

- First-name, middle-name, inner-city, super-man

- However, JavaScript does not allow hyphens. The hypens aer going to be reserved for subtraction only.

Underscore

- Middle_name super_man last_name

Camel case

- Like a camel has two humps, in the camel case, you are going to make the first letter of each name capitalized.

- MiddleName SuperMan LastName

- However, many programmers turn it around so that the first letter is lowercased while the second letter is capitalized.

- middleName superMan lastName

Character set

- JavaScript uses a Unicode character set.

- Unicode is going to cover a majority of any character, symbol, or punctuation that you are going to see in the world.

Chapter 9:
Enabling and Disabling JavaScript

- JavaScript is a program that is going to be supported by various browsers such as Firefox, Google Chrome, Internet Explorer and many more.

- Almost everyone uses JavaScript so there really is no way to not have it installed on your browser, however, there are some people that are concerned about JavaScript abusing its privileges and being used by site owners that are less than reputable, so there are those who decide that they want to disable JavaScript instead of allowing it to be used on their browser.

- When JavaScript is used is going to be based on the web pages that you visit that are going to demonstrate that the information you are putting into it is important or not. The importance is going to be determined by your web browser and your computer.

Internet Explorer 7 and 8

- First you are going to open up the "tools" menu.

- Next you will select the "internet options" so that the internet options dialog box is opened in a separate window.

- From here, you will click on the security tab

- After that you are going to click on the internet symbol. Most of the time this is going to be the globe.

- Now, you will click on "custom level", so that the security settings box is opened.

- Under the settings list, you will scroll down until you see "scripting"

- In scripting, you are going to select the radio button that is just to the left of enabled. This is going to cause a dot to appear therefore enabling JavaScript. If you are wanting to disable it, then you will select disable.

- For any other settings that you may be unsure about, you need to check with the network administrator so that you are not messing something up.

- Now that you have enabled or disabled JavaScript, you will click "OK" so that the security settings box closes.

- Be sure to click on "Yes," when the warning box appears.

- "Click on OK once more, and your internet options box will be closed.

Internet Explorer 6

- Open the tools menu

- Open your internet options dialog box by selecting internet options

- Select the security tab.

- Click on the globe for your internet options

- Go to the custom level so that the security settings dialog box opens

- Move down to scripting so that you can enable or disable JavaScript.

- Click "OK" so that the security settings box closes.

- "Click "Yes" on the warning box.

- And finally, click "Ok" to close the internet options box.

FireFox

- Open the tools menu if you are using Windows or the Firefox menu if you have the OS X system.

- Depending on which system you are using, you are either going to select options or preferences so that, that dialog box opens.

- You will now see a row of colored icons; you will need to select the content one.

- Make sure that the box that is to the left of Enable JavaScript is ticked, or not if you are wanting JavaScript disabled.

- Click "OK" and the box will be closed.

Google Chrome

- Click on the spanner icon that is located at the top right of the menu.

- Select options so that the Google Chrome options dialog box opens.

- Within the Google Chrome options, you are going to click the "under the bonnet" tab.

- This will open up the privacy section where you are going to click on the content settings button.

- In the content settings you will click on "JavaScript" which you are going to find listed in the features box.

- You can either click on allow it to run on all sites, which is highly recommended, or you can click on "do not allow any site to run JavaScript" so that it becomes disabled.

- Close the content settings box

- Close the Google Chrome options box.

Opera

- Open the file menu for version six or the tools menu for versions seven through nine.

- Hover over the quick preferences button.

- In the submenu that pops u, click on enable so that you can enable or disable JavaScript.

- In the event that you are using a Mac OS X then you are going to need to select quick preferences in the Opera menu instead of clicking on the one in the tools menu.

Safari

- If you are using OS X open the Safari menu, if you are using Windows, open the edit menu. Should the menu not be visible then press the ALT key on your keyboard.

- Click on preferences

- Once that has opened, you will click on the security icon, this may appear as a padlock.

- Inside of the web content section, you are going to check the "Enable JavaScript" box if you want it enabled, if you do not, then uncheck it.

- Close all of your dialog boxes by clicking on the red button that appears at the top left or right of the page.

Camino

- Open the Camino menu

- Click on preferences so that a dialog box is opened

- Select web features

- In the content control section, you are going to see the enable JavaScript button. If you want it enabled, make sure it is clicked. If not, then unclick it.

- Close the dialog box by use of the red button at the top left.

SeaMonkey

- Open the edit menu in Windows or the SeaMonkey menu on OS X

- Select preferences so that the preference box opens.

- Inside of the category list, you are going to want to select the plus sign beside advanced. A list is going to appear under it.

- In the scripts and plug-ins list, the JavaScript option is going to be found. Click it if you want it enabled, unclick it if you do not want it enabled.

- Click okay and the preference box will be closed.

Internet Explorer 4.x or 5.x on Windows

- Open the tools menu.

- Select internet options.

- Open the security tab.

- Click on the internet symbol (the globe)

- Click on the custom level button.

- In the settings list, you are going to find scripting

- Under active scripting, you are going to be able to enable or disable JavaScript.

- Click on "Ok"

- Select "Yes" on the warning box

- Click "Ok" to close out all boxes.

Internet Explorer 4.x or 5.x on Mac

- Open the edit menu on OS 9 or the Explorer menu on OS X

- Click on the preference button.

- In the list located on the left, click on web browser so that the bullets can be seen underneath it.

- Click on web content

- In the active content part, you are going to click on the box next to enable scripting. If you want to disable it, then make sure there is no tick mark.

Netscape 4.6 or 6.x on Windows or Mac

- Open up the edit menu

- Click on the preference button

- Go to the category list and select advanced

- In the list on the right, you can enable JavaScript by placing a tick mark in the box. If you want it disabled, then untick the box.

- Click "Ok"

Netscape 3.x on Windows

- Open up the options menu

- Click on network preferences

- Inside of the preference dialog box, click on the language tab

- Check the box so that there is a tick next to enable JavaScript, if you want it disabled, then uncheck the box.

- Click "Ok"

Netscape 2.x on Windows

- Open up the options menu

- Select the security preferences

- In the dialog box that opens, click on the general tab.

- Click on the check box next to disable JavaScript to enable JavaScript, or again so that you can disable it.

- Click "Ok"

Chapter 10:
JavaScript's Placement

- JavaScript offers flexibility for where the code can be placed in an HTML document.

- The way that is preferred is going to include the JavaScript into the HTML file like this:

Script in <head> will be </head>

Script in the <body> will be </body>

Script in the <body> </body> and <head> </head> section

Section in an external file in the <head> section is </head>

JavaScript in the <head> </head> section

- If you want the script to run based on an event, such as the user clicking on something, then you are going to need to place this script into the head section.

```
<html>

<head>

<script type = "text/javascript">

<! –

Function sayHello() {

Alert("Hello Earth")

}

// - - >

</script>

</head>

<body>

<input type = "button" onclick =" sayHello()" value = "Say Hello" />

</body>

</html>
```

- The output for this is going to be Hello Earth

JavaScript in <body> and </body> sections

- Should you need to run script as the page loads, the script is going to generate the content on the page as the script goes into the <body> portion of the document.

- If you do not have any functions defined when using JavaScript.

Example

<html>

<head>

</head>

<body>

<script type = "text/javascript">

<! - -

Document.write ("Hello Universe")

// - - >

</script>

<p> This is web page body </p>

</body>

</html>

- The result for this cod is going to be:

Hello Universe.

This is web page body.

JavaScript in <body> and <head> sections

- JavaScript can be placed into the code in the <head> and <body> sections at the same time.

Example

<html>

<head>

<script type = "text/javascript">

<! - -

Function sayHello() {

Alert ("Hello people of Earth")

}

```
// - - >

</script>

</head>

<body>

<script type = "text/javascript">

<! - -

Document.write( "Hello people of Earth")

// - - >

</script>

<input type = "button" onclick = "sayHello()"
value = "Say Hello" />

</body>

</html>
```

- Your result is going to be Hello people of Earth.

JavaScript in external files

- When working more extensively with JavaScript, there are going to be some cases that you are going to end up using code that is identical across multiple pages on a site.

- You do not have to be restricted to maintaining identical code in multiple HTML files.

- Script tags are going to provide you with a mechanism that will allow you to store JavaScript in an external file and then proceed to include it in an HTML file.

- This example is going to include an external JavaScript file in the HTML code through the use of script tags and an src attribute.

Example

<html>

<head>

<script type = "text/javascript" src = "filename.js" ></script>

```
</head>

<body>

.....

</body>

</html>
```

- When using JavaScript in an external file, you will need to write out all of the JavaScript source code into a text file with the extension of .js.

- This example will keep the same content in the file from file.js and you will use sayHello in the HTML file once you have included the file.js file.

Example

Function sayHello() {

Alert ("Hello son")

}

Chapter 11:
Variables in JavaScript

- Variables are basically small boxes with names tagged to them.

- Variables are places for you to store things

- The name on your box is going to be the variables name

- Each box is going to have contents that are going to pertain to the variable.

- Think of it like your computer's memory. Information is stored on the memory like the contents of the variables.

- Any variable is going to refer to what name you assign to it.

Example

<html>

<head>

<title> My Javascript Page </title>

</head>

```
<body>

<script>

Myname = "Susann" ;

Document.write(myname) ;

</script>

</body>

</html>
```

- If you want your text to be stored in the variable, then the text needs to be inside of a set of quotes.

- As mentioned previously, this is so the program can tell your variable and normal text apart.

Example

```
<html>

<head>

<title> My Javascript Page </title>

</head>
```

```
<body>

<script>

Susann = "my first name" ;

Myname = Susann ;

Document.write (myname) ;

</script>

</body>

</html>
```

- Your output will be:

  - First line: the Susann variable

  - Second line: Susann will be stored for the variable myname

  - Third line: myname will be inserted into the document

  - The end result will be that "my first name" will be placed on the page.

Assigning Values to Variables

- One of the most common ways to assign a value is going to be to use the equals sign (=)

Arithmetic Operators

- There are some operators such as a++ and even a—that you are going to be able to live without.

- This is because you are going to be able to use other operators to do the same thing that these operators do.

- However, they are going to be often used in scripting because they are faster to type then adding a = a+1.

- The operator ++ is going to be used for increments. For example if a = 5 and you enter a++ then a is now going to equal 6.

- -- is going to be a decrement. Just like the example above, if a is 5 and you type in a—then you are now going to have 4.

- The percentage sing (%) is going to return the modulus of whatever is left after you have divided 2 numbers. So, if you do the operation 8 % 3; you are going to get a remainder of 2.

Comparing Variables

- You can use several different variations in order to compare variables.

- However, the simplest way to do it is to use a double equals sign (==)

- So if (a == z) then ("a equals z")

- In the event that you forget to use a double equal sign when you are trying to compare variables, then you can use a single equals sign as well. But, you will not be comparing variables.

- Instead, the variable that appears on the left side of your equals sign is going to be assigned as the value for the variable that is on the right side.

Example

If (firstname = "Susann") {alert("Nice name!!!")}

- You find that this is a common but that is going to end up running your script.

- If you have used Python, then you know the operators and what they mean. However, if you have not, then here are the operators that you can use in order to compare to different variables.

  - == equals to

  - != not equal to

  - < less than

  - > greater than

  - <= less than or equal to

  - >= greater than or equal to

Chapter 12:
Operators Used in JavaScript

- An expression is going to have an operand and an operator. The operands are going to be the numbers in the expression and the operator is going to be the arithmetic sign.

- There are several types of operators that JavaScript supports.

  o   Conditional operators

  o   Arithmetic operators

  o   Assignment operators

  o   Comparison operators

  o   Logical operators.

Arithmetic Operators

- Addition (+): two operands are going to be added together.

- Subtraction (-): the second operand is going to be subtracted from the first.

- Multiplication (*): both operands are going to be multiplied.

- Division (/): the numerator is going to be divided by the denominator.

- Modulus (%): the output is going to be the remainder of the integer from division.

- Increment (+ +): the integer is going to be increased by a value of one.

- Decrement (- -): the integer will be decreased by a value of one.

Example

<html>

<body>

<script type = "text/javascript">

<! - -

Var a = 33;

Var b = 10;

Var c = "test";

```
Var linebreak = "<br />";

Document.write("a + b =");

Result = a + b;

Document.write (result) ;

Document.write(linebreak);

Document.write (" a – b = ");

Result = a – b;

Document.write(result);

Document.write(linebreak);

Document.write("a / b = ");

Result = a / b;

Document.write(result);

Document.write(linebreak);

Document.write(" a % b = ");

Result = a % b;

Document.write(result);

Document.write(linebreak);
```

```
Document.write( "a + b + c = ");

Result = a + b + c;

Document.write(result);

Document.write(linebreak);

A = ++a;

Document.write ("++a = ");

Result = ++a;

Document.write(result);

Document.write(linebreak);

B = --b

Document.write(" - - b = ");

Result = - - b;

Document.write(result);

Document.write(linebreak);

// - - >

< / script>
```

Set the variables to a different value and try it yourself.

</body>

</html>

- Your output is going to be:

A + b = 43

A – b = 23

A / b = 3.3

A % b = 3

A + b + c = 43Test

++a = 35

-- b = 8

Comparison Operators

- Equal (= =): the value of the two operands are going to be check to see if they are equal or not. If they are, then the condition is going to be true.

- Not equal (!=): if the two values are check to see that they are equal and they prove to not be equal, then the condition is going to be true.

- Greater than (>): the left operand should be greater than the right operand, if it is, then the condition will be true.

- Less than (<): if the left operand is less than the value on the right, the condition is going to be true.

- Greater than or equal to (> =): the left operand is going to be greater than or equal to the value that is found on the right. If it is, then the condition is going to be true.

- Less than or equal to (< =): the left operand should be less than or equal to the value on the right. If it is, then the condition is going to be true.

Example

<html>

<body>

<script type = "text/javascript">

```
<! - -

Var a = 10;

Var b = 20;

Var linebreak = "<br />";

Document.write( "(a == b) => ");

Result = ( a == b);

Document.write(result);

Document.write(linebreak);

Document.write( " (a < b) => ");

Result = (a < b);

Document.write(result);

Document.write(linebreak);

Document.write( " (a > b) => " );

Result = (a > b);

Document.write(result);

Document.write(linebreak);

Document.write ( " (a != b) => ");
```

```
Result = a != b);

Document.write(result);

Document.write(linebreak);

Document.write( " (a >= b) => ");

Result = ( a >= b);

Document.write(result);

Document.write(linebreak);

Document.write( " (a <= b) => ");

Result = (a <= b);

Document.write(result);

Document.write(linebreak);

// - - >

</script>

</body>

</html>
```

- The output for this example is going to be:

(a == b) = false

(a < b) = true

(a > b) = false

(a != b) = true

(a >= b) = false

(a <= b) = true

Logical operators

- Logical AND (&&): both the operands should be non-zero. If they are, then the condition is going to be true.

- Logical OR (||): should one of the operands be non-zero, then the condition will be true.

- Logical NOT (!): the logical state will be reversed based on the state of the oerpand. If the condition is true, then the logical NOT is going to make it false.

Example

<html>

<body>

```
<script type = "text/javascript">

<! - -

Var a = true;

Var b = false;

Var linebreak = "<br />";

Document.write (" (a && b) => ");

Result = (a && b);

Document.write(result);

Document.write(linebreak);

Document.write (" (a || b) = > ");

Result = (a || b);

Document.write(result);

Document.write(linebreak);

Document.write( "! (a && b) => ");

Result = (! (a && b));

Document.write(result);

Document.write(lionebreak);
```

// - - >

</script>

</body>

</html>

- The results for this example is going to be:

(a && b) = false

(a || b) = true

!(a && b) = true

Bitwise Operators

- Bitwise AND (&): a Boolean value will be performed AND the operation for each bit with its individual integer arguments.

- Bitwise OR (|): the Boolean will be performed or the operation for each integer.

- Bitwise XOR (^): the Boolean exclusive will be performed or the operation for each bit in tis integer arguments. The exclusive or means that either the operand on the right or the operand on the left will be true, however, both will not be true.

- Bitwise Not (~): an unary operator that will operate by reversing all the bits that are in the operand.

- Left shift (<<): all of the bits in the first operand will be moved to the left by the number of places that are specified by the second operand. The new bits are going to be filled in with zeros. When everything is shifted to the left by one, the equivalent is going to multiply it by two, therefore shifting it two positions will be equivalent to multiplying it by four.

- Right shift (>>): the binary will be shifted right y the number of bits that has been specified by the right operand.

- Right shift with zero (>>>): the operand is going to be exactly like a right shift, but the bits that are going to be shifted on the left will always be zero.

Example:

<html>

<body>

```
<script type = "text/javascript">

<! –

Var a = 2; // bit is going to be presented as 10

Var b = 3; // bit will be presented as 11

Var linebreak = "<br />";

Document.write (" (a & b => ");

Result = (a & b);

Document.write(result);

Document.write(linebreak);

Document.write (" (a | b) => ");

Result = ( a | b);

Document.write(result);

Document.write(linebreak);

Document.write(" (a ^ b) => ");

Result = (a ^ b);

Document.write(result);

Document.write(linebreak);
```

```
Document.write(" (~b) => ");

Result = (~b);

Document.write(result);

Document.write(linebreak);

Document.write(" (a << b) => ");

Result (a << b);

Document.write(result);

Document.write(linebreak);

Document.write(" (a >> b) => ");

Result = (a >> b);

Document.write(result);

Document.write(linebreak);

//- - >

</script>

</body>

</html>
```

- Results:

(a & b) = 2

(a | b) = 3

(a ^ b) = 1

(~b) = -4

(a << b) = 16

(a >> b) = 0

Assignment Operators

- Simple assignment (=): the value from the right side is going to be assigned to the left.

- Add and assignment (+ =): the right operand will be added to the left and the value will then be added to the left.

- Subtract and assignment (- =): the right will be subtracted from the left, and the resulting value will be assigned to the left.

- Multiply and assignment (* =): the operand on the right will be multiplied by the operand on the left. The value will then be assigned to the left operand.

- Divide and assignment (/ =): the left operand is going to be divided by the right while the result is assigned to the left.

- Modulus and assignment (% =) : the modulus will be taken from the two operands and then assign the value to the left.

- There is some logic that applies to the bitwise operators so that they ultimately become <<=, >>= , >>=, &=, |= as well as ^=.

Example

<html>

<body>

<script type = "text/javascript">

<! - -

Var a = 33;

Var b = 10;

Var linebreak = "<br />";

Document.write("value of a => (a = b) => ");

```
Result = (a = b);

Document.write(result);

Document.write(linebreak);

Document.write ("Valeu of a => (a += b) => ");

Result = (a += b);

Document.write(result);

Document.write(linebreak);

Document.write (" Value of a => (a *= b) => ");

Result = (a *= b);

Document.write(result);

Document.write(linebreak);

Document.write(" Value of a => (a /= b) => ");

Result = (a /= b);

Document.write(result);

Document.write(linebreak);

Document.write ("Value of a => (a %= b) => ");

Result = (a %= b);
```

Document.write(result);

Document.write(linebreak);

// - ->

</script>

</body>

</html>

- Output:

Value of a => (a =b) = 10

Value of a => (a += b) = 20

Value of a => (a -=b) = 10

Value of a => (a *= b) = 100

Value of a => (a /= b) = 10

Value of a => (a %= b) = 0

Miscellaneous Operator

- There are two operators that are going to be useful when you are learning JavaScript. They are the conditional operator (? :) and the typeof operator.

Conditional Operator

- The conditional operator is going to evaluate the expression to see if it has a true or false value before it executes one of the two statements that are given depending on the result that it gets after it is evaluated.

- Conditional (? :): if the condition is true then do the statement with the value of x. if it is not, do the other statement.

Example

<html>

<body>

<script type = "text/javascript">

<! - -

Var a = 10;

Var b = 20;

Var linebreak = "<br />";

Document.write (" ((a >b) ? 100 : 200) => ");

Result = (a > b) ? 100 : 200;

Document.write(result);

Document.write(linebreak);

Document.write (" ((a < b) ? 100 : 200) => ");

Result = (a < b) ? 100 : 200;

Document.write(result);

Document.write(linebreak);

// - - >

</script>

</body>

</html>

- The results are:

((a >) ? 100 : 200 => 200

((a < b) ? 100 : 200 => 100

Typeof Operator

- The typeof operator is known as a unary operator. It is placed before the single operand, which is going to be any type of operand.

- The value is going to be a string that will indicate which data type has been used.

- The typeof operator is going evaluate Boolean, string, or numbers only if the value is returned true or false based on the evaluation.

- The list below is going to give the value that is returned from the typeof operator.

- Number = number

- Null = object

- String = string

- Boolean = Boolean

- Undefined = undefined

- Function = function

- Object = object.

Example

<html>

<body>

<script type "text/javascript">

```
<! - -

Var  a = 10

Var b = "String";

Var linebreak = "<br />";

Result = (typeof b == "string" ? "B is String" : "B
is Numeric");

Document.write( "Result => ");

Document.write(result);

Document.write(linebreak);

Result = (typeof a == "string" ? "A is String" : "A
is Numeric");

Document.write("result => ");

Document.write(result);

Document.write(linebreak);

// - ->

</script>

</body>

</html>
```

- Results

Result => B is String

Result => A is Numeric

Chapter 13:
Decision Making with JavaScript

Description

Have you ever seen that annoying pop up box that tells you that your JavaScript needs to be updated? Have you ever wondered what JavaScript does for your computer?

In this book, not only are you going to learn exactly what JavaScript does, but you are going to learn how to use it.

You will also make yourself a much more marketable asset for any business and increase your paycheck dramatically by mastering the strategies we teach.

Here is a Preview of What You Will Discover:

- JavaScript Syntax

- Decision making with JavaScript

- The operators that are used in JavaScript

- Variables in JavaScript

- JavaScript functions

- How to write your own program with JavaScript

- And so much more.

Don't wait any longer to start mastering this powerful Programming language!

- If you have experience in any other programming language, then you know that there are usually statements that are used for decision making. JavaScript is no different.

If statement

- The if statement will be used in order to check for conditions to see if they are true or not.

- The condition can be any expression that will be returned true or false.

- If a statement satisfies the statement, then the statement will be executed.

Syntax

If(condition)

{

Statement 3

Statement 4

...

}

- If there is only one statement that has to be executed after the if condition, then you are not going to need the curly brackets ({}).

- If there is more than one statement, then the brackets are going to be necessary.

Syntax

If(condition)

Statement

- However, it is going to be recommended that you use the curly brackets so that your code is easier to understand and manage.

Example

<script>

If (6 > 2)

{

Document.write("yes 6 is greater than 2");

Document.write "<br />" + "JavaScript is easy");

Document.write("<br />");

}

- Output

Yes 6 is greater than 2.

JavaScript is easy.

Example

If(true)

Document.write ("Ah! A Boolean inside condition. Also, I am not using curly brackets");

// it does work without having to use curly brackets

- Output

Ah! A Boolean inside condition. Also, I am not using curly brackets.

Example

If (2 == 4)

{

Document.write ("This is not going to be printed");

}

//since the condition has turned out to be false, the statement is not going to be executed.

</script>

Else statement

- The else statement is going to be used with the if statement.

- When the condition fails, the else statement is going to be executed.

Syntax

If(condition)

{

Statements

}

Else

{

Statements

}

- The curly brackets can be drops when using the else statement. But only if there is a single statement that has to be executed.

Example

<script>

If 5 > 7

{

Document.write("True");

}

Else

{

Document.write("False");

}

- The output is going to be false.

Else if statement

- If there are a variety of conditions that you have to check, you can use a multitude of if statements in order to do this.

- All of the if conditions are going to be checked one at a time.

- If a single condition satisfies it, then it will not continue to perform further checks.

- This is when an else if statement comes into play

Syntax

If(condition)

{

Statements

}

Else if (condition)

{

Statements

}

Else

{

Statements

}

- When every condition ends up failing, the final else statement is going to be executed.

Example

```
<script>

Var a = 3;

Var b = 4;

If (a > b)

{

Document.write(" a is greater than b");
```

```
}

Else if (a < b)

{

Document.write(" a is smaller than b");

}

Else

{

Document.write("Nothing worked");

}

</script>
```

Switch statement

- A switch statement is going to do the same task that the else if statement is going to do.

- A switch statement is going to be used when the conditions are more.

- This is going to be because the switch statement is going to perform better than the else if statement will.

Syntax

Switch(expression)

{

Case value -1: statements; break;

Case value -2: statements; break;

Case value 3: statements; break;

....

Case value-n: statements; break;

Default: statements; break;

}

- The switch statement is going to evaluate the expression to see if it matches with any case.

- In the event that it matches, then the statement inside of that case is going to be executed being followed by a break statement.

- The break statement is going to make sure that no other case statement executed.

- If the expression does not match any case value, then the default case is going to be executed.

- The can be a variety of statements.

- There is no need to use curly brackets inside of a case construct.

- The break statement can also be omitted in the default construct should the default be the last statement in the switch.

Example

```
<script>

Var a = 8

Switch(a)

{

Case 1: document.write("one"); break;

Case 2: document.write( "two"); break;

Case 3: document.write( "three"); break;

Case 4: document.write( "four"); break;

Case 5: document.write( "five"); break;
```

Default: document.write("number not found");

}

// outputs five

</script>

- The case value can be any number, string, or character.

Example

<script>

Var I = 'j';

Switch(i)

{

Case 'a': document.write("a found"); break;

Case 'b': document.write('b found"); break;

Case 'c': document.write("c found"); break;

Case 'j': document.write("j found"); break;

Case 'string': document.write("string found"); break;

Default: document.write("nothing found");

```
}
```

//outputs j found

</script>

Ternary operator (?:)

- The ternary operator is the operator that most programmers are going to use.

- It is composed of three operands.

Syntax

Condition ? if-true-execute-this : if-false-execute-this;

- Should the condition go right, then the statement that is placed before the colon is going to be executed.

- If the statement is false, then the statement after the colon is going to be executed.

- A multitude of statements are not going to be allowed.

- However, multiple statements can be executed through the use of a function and then calling the function should the condition be true or false.

Example

<script>

True ? document.write ("True value found") : document.write("False value found");

Document.write("<br />");

// outputs True value found.

(6 > 5 && 3 == 2) ? document.write("True") : document.write("False");

Document.write("
");

// outputs False

Var a = (true) ? 1 : 2;

Document.write(a);

//outputs 1

</script>

Nested if else and switch statements

- You have the ability to insert an if, or, else, or even a switch condition inside of another condition.

- This is known as nesting

- You can nest an if, else, or switch condition to any number of level, but your code is going to end up being more confusing.

Syntax

If(condition)

{

If (other condition)

{

Statements;

}

}

Else

{

```
If (other condition)

{

Statements;

}

Else

{

Switch(expression)

{

Case value-1: statements; break;

...

}

}

}
```

Chapter 14:
Events

- There is an interaction between JavaScript and HTML that is handled through events that will occur whenever the user or the browser manipulates the page.

- As a page loads, this is called an event.

- Whenever a user selects a button, this is known as an event as well.

- Other event examples are pressing keys, closing windows, and resizing windows.

- A developer can use these events so that JavaScript's code can be executed which is going to cause the buttons to close the windows while a message is displayed to the user. The data is going to be validated and there will virtually any type of response imaginable.

- Events are part of a DOM (Document Object Model) level three. Every HTML element that is confined within a set of events is going to trigger the JavaScript code.

Onclick event

- This is going to be the most frequently used event.

- This is going to happen whenever the user clicks the left button on their mouse.

- You have the ability as the developer to put a warning, validation, or anything else against this event type.

Example

<html>

<head>

<script type = "text/javascript">

<! - -

Function sayHello() {

Alert ("Hello love")

}

// - - >

```
</script>

</head>

<body>

<p> click on the button and see the results </p>

<form>

<input type = "button" onclick =" sayHello()"
value = "Say Hello" />

</form>

</body>

</html>
```

- Output: Hello love

Onsubmit Event

- An omsubmit even will occur whenever you try to submit a form.

- The form can have a validation against this event.

Example

```
<html>
```

```
<head>

<script type = "text/javascript">

<! - -

Function validation() {

All validation goes here

...

Return either true or false

}

// - - >

</script>

</head>

<body>

<form method = "POST" action = "t. cgi"
onsubmit = "return validate()">

...

<input type = "submit" value = "Submit" />

</form>
```

```
</body>

</html>
```

Onmouseover and onmouseout

- There are two events that help to create nice effects with the images or text

- Theonmouseover will trigger whenever the mouse is brought over the element.

- The onmouseout will be triggered when the mouse is moved out of the element.

Example

```
<html>

<head>

<script type = "text/javascript">

<! - -

Function over() {

Document.write("Mouse Over");

}

Fuction.out() {
```

Document.write ("Mouse Out");

}

// - ->

</script>

</head>

<body>

<p> Bring your mouse inside the division to see the result: </p>

<div onmouseover = "over()" onmouseout = "out()">

<h2> This is inside the division </h2>

</div>

</body>

</html>

- The result is going to be Mouse Over

HTML 5 Standard Events

- HTM 5 events are going to be listed in this section.

- Offline: triggered whenever a document goes offline

- Onabort: an abort event has been triggered.

- Onafterprint: triggered after the document has been printed

- Onbeforeonload: triggers after a document has been loaded.

- Onbeforeprint: triggered before the document has been printed.

- Onblur: triggered once the window has lost focus.

- Oncanplay: whenever media starts playing, it may have to be stopped before it has a chance to buffer.

- Oncanplaythrough: the media is going to play without having to stop to buffer.

- Onchange: an element has been changed.

- Onclick: the mouse has been clicked.

- Oncontextmenu: the context menu is triggered.

- ondblclicK: the mouse has been double-clicked.

- Ondrag: an element on the screen has been dragged.

- Ondragend: the end of a drag operation.

- Ondragenter: the element has been moved to a valid drop spot.

- Ondragleave: the element has been dragged over to a valid drop target.

- Ondragover: this is triggered at the start of the drag operation

- Ondragstart: this is also triggered at the start of the drag operation.

- Ondrop: the element will have been dropped.

- Ondurationchange: the length of the media has been changed.

- Onemptied: the media source becomes empty suddenly.

- Onended: the media has reached its end.

- Onerror: an error has occurred.

- Onfocus: the window is focused.

- Onformchange: the form has been changed.

- Onforminput: the form gets input from the user

- Onhaschanged: the document has been changed.

- Oninput: the element has been given input from the user.

- Oninvalid: the element has been found invalid.

- Onkeydown: a key has been pressed

- Onkeypress: a key was pressed and then released

- Onkeyup: the key was released after being pressed

- Onload: the document has been loaded.

- Onloadeddata: the media data has been loaded.

- Onloadmetadata: the duration and other meta data has been loaded from the media element.

- Onloadstart: the browser has been started and media data has been loaded.

- Onmessage: a message is triggered.

- Onmousedown: the mouse button has been pressed.

- Onmousemove: the mouse has been moved

- Onmouseout: the mouse pointer moves out of the element.

- Onmouseover: the mouse moves over the element

- Onmouseup: the mouse button is released

- Onmousewheel: the mouse wheel has been rotated

- Onoffline: the document has gone offline

- Ononline: the document has come online

- Onpagehide: the window has been hidden

- Onpageshow: the window has now become visable.

- Onpause: the media player has been paused.

- Onplay: the media player is now playing.

- Onpopstate: the window's history has been changed.

- Onprogress: the browser is searching for the media data

- Onratechange: the media's data playing rate has been changed.

- Onreadystatechange: the ready-state has been changed.

- Onredo: the document has been instructed to perform a redo.

- Onresize: the window has been resized.

- Onscroll: the scrollbar has been scrolled up or down.

- Onseeked: the media's elements seeking attribute has no longer been found as true, therefore the seeking has been ended.

- Onseeking: the media's element's seeking attribute is found as true and is still seeking.

- Onselect: the element has been selected

- Onstalled: there has been an error found in the fetching media.

- Onstorage: the document has been loaded.

- Onsubmit: a form has been submitted.

- Onsuspend: the browser has started to search for the media's data, but has stopped before the entire file has been able to be found.

- Ontimeupdate: the media has changed the playing position.

- Onundo: the document has been told to perform an undo.

- Onunload; the user has left the document.

- Onvolumechange: the media has changed volume or has been set to mute.

- Onwaiting: the media has stopped playing, but will resume.

Chapter 15:
Page Printing

- There may be times that you want a button placed on your web page so that you can print the contents of that page through an actual printer. JavaScript helps to make this a reality by using the print function for a window object.

- The JavaScript print function window.print() will print the page yo are currently on.

- This function can be called on by using the onclick event

Example

<html>

<head>

<script type = "text/javascript">

<! - -

// - - >

</script>

```
</head>

<body>

<form>

<input type = "button" value = "Print" onclick =
"window.print()" />

</form>

</body>

<html>
```

- It will serve the purpose of getting a printout, this is not the way that is recommended to get a page to print.

- A printer friendly page is just a page that has text and no images of any kind.

- To make a page printer friendly you can:

    o Make a copy of the page to leave out images and text that you do not want on the page.

    o If you do not want an extra copy of the page, you are able to mark the printable text by using the proper comments such as <! – PRINT

STARTS HERE - - > <! - - PRINT
ENDS HERE - - >

How to print a page

- Should the steps not work for you on a web page, then you are able to use the browser's standard toolbar in order to print the web page.

- Use the file path: file – print – click OK

Conclusion

Thank you again for purchasing this book!

I hope this book was able to help you to learn what JavaScript is and how you are going to be able to use it so that you can create your own script.

The next step is to take what you have learned and practice it. With what you have learned in this book, you are going to be able to create your own web pages and applications.

Additionally, please visit our Amazon Author page for more great info and resources.

https://www.amazon.com/author/ma1982

You will find all the books you need to learn about:

Python Programming, SQL, JavaScript, and even **TOR** if that's something you fancy!!

https://www.amazon.com/HACKING-Beginner-Penetration-Security-Programming-ebook/dp/B01N8ZF5F4

https://www.amazon.com/PYTHON-Beginner-Practical-Programming-Beginners-ebook/dp/B01N91WKHD

https://www.amazon.com/dp/B01MSLLTYR

Last but not least, if you enjoyed this book and thought it was helpful, we certainly won't say no to a 5-star **review on Amazon**.

Thank You and Best of Luck in Your JavaScript Programming Endeavors!!!

www.ingramcontent.com/pod-product-compliance
Lightning Source LLC
Chambersburg PA
CBHW071127050326
40690CB00008B/1367